T0101935

NONBINARY
BIRD OF PARADISE

AKRON SERIES IN POETRY

AKRON SERIES IN POETRY

Mary Biddinger, Editor

For a complete listing of titles published in the series,
go to www.uakron.edu/uapress/poetry

NONBINARY
BIRD OF PARADISE

EMILIA PHILLIPS

 The University of Akron Press
Akron, Ohio

ISBN: 978-1-62922-276-9 (paper)
ISBN: 978-1-62922-277-6 (ePDF)
ISBN: 978-1-62922-278-3 (ePub)

A catalog record for this title is available from the Library of Congress.

∞ The paper used in this publication meets the minimum requirements of ANSI/NISO Z39.48–1992
(Permanence of Paper).

Cover image: General Research Division, The New York Public Library. "Common Mocking
Bird, 1. Males 2. Female (Florida Jessamine. Gelseminum niditum. Rattlesnake.)" New York Public
Library Digital Collections. https://digitalcollections.nypl.org/items/510d47d9-72a9-a3d9-e040-
e00a18064a99. Cover design by Amy Freels.

Marianne Boruch, excerpt from "In Dürer's Engraving" from *The Anti-Grief.* Copyright © 2019 by
Marianne Boruch. Reprinted with the permission of The Permissions Company, LLC on behalf of
Copper Canyon Press, coppercanyonpress.org.

Mahmoud Darwish, excerpt from "A State of Siege" from *The Butterfly's Burden*, translated by Fady
Joudah. Copyright © 2007 by Mahmoud Darwish. Translation copyright © 2007 by Fady Joudah.
Reprinted with the permission of The Permissions Company, LLC on behalf of Copper Canyon
Press, coppercanyonpress.org.

"Kissing God Goodbye" from *Directed by Desire: The Complete Poems of June Jordan*, Copper Canyon
Press © Christopher D. Meyer, 2007. Reprinted by permission of the Frances Goldin Literary Agency.

Excerpt(s) from THE WORLD AND OTHER PLACES: STORIES by Jeanette Winterson,
copyright © 1998 by Jeanette Winterson. Used by permission of Alfred A. Knopf, an imprint of the
Knopf Doubleday Publishing Group, a division of Penguin Random House LLC. All rights reserved.

Nonbinary Bird of Paradise was designed and typeset in Garamond with Futura titles by Amy Freels
and printed on sixty-pound natural and bound by Bookmasters of Ashland, Ohio.

Produced in conjunction with the University of
Akron Affordable Learning Initiative.
More information is available at
www.uakron.edu/affordablelearning/.

—for Claudia Cabello Hutt

CONTENTS

You mean to tell me that the planet
is a brainchild
of a single
male
head of household?
—JUNE JORDAN, "KISSING GOD GOODBYE"

When I see a word held hostage to manhood, I have to rescue it.
—JEANETTE WINTERSON, "THE POETICS OF SEX"

For Occupation – This –
The spreading wide my narrow Hands
To gather Paradise –
—EMILY DICKINSON, "I DWELL IN POSSIBILITY – (466)"

1

BAKER & TAYLOR
PUBLISHER SERVICES

BAKER & TAYLOR PUBLISHER SERVICES
30 AMBERWOOD PKWY
ASHLAND, OH 44805
Phone: 419-281-1802

Sales Order

February 16, 2024

BO433213

Sold To:

BAKER & TAYLOR BOOKS
PO BOX 8888
MOMENCE, IL 60954

ACCT #   233

Ship To:

BAKER & TAYLOR BOOKS
251 MT OLIVE CHURCH ROAD
COMMERCE, GA 30599
Phone: 7049983265
ACCT #   204

Pub #51900

PURCHASE ORDER NO.		SHIP VIA	FREIGHT TERMS
COM212B249		BAKER & TAYLOR COLLECT	Collect (Account)

Quantity	Part Number	Description	Unit Price
		***** BACK ORDER RELEASE ******	
		THANK YOU FOR YOUR ORDER!	
		*****	
3	9781629222769	NONBINARY BIRD OF PARADISE	$16.95

Total Wgt: .90

** PACKING SLIP ONLY **
INVOICE SENT SEPARATELY

Thank you for your business!

If you have any questions concerning missing or damaged items, please contact the number above. All UPS and FedEx packages are insured, however, you must save the original shipping container and any packing material in order to file a claim. Notification must be made within 10 days of receipt.

THE QUEERNESS OF EVE

"Pre-unbearable."
—MARIANNE BORUCH, "IN DÜRER'S ENGRAVING"

A rib-wife's birthright: anxiety
of influence and some guy's
leech-kiss. No choice
but *yes* when there's a world to be
blooded. Birth was painless at first
but my ladybits still turned into an inside-out
fig. Say *apple* used to mean all fruit but say *no*
language yet, say *therefore conversational*
in silence. That's how it went.
Imagine smalltalk when the weather's perfect.
Imagine how quick he came the first time
Man had sex. You probably guessed
I created the female orgasm
all by my lonesome.
Where did the time go?
Can I say I wasted it
watching the boring anachronisms
rutting in a clearing, before I came upon two
swollen bonobos legging furiously
as if their blades were dull,
as if they invented gravity that could pull
down stars? I've seen novas fall
from the Garden's ramparts,
seen the tsunamis they make
of the primordial
soup. I was always hungry
for something the Garden couldn't tender, knowledge
stripteasing like a poppy, some blousy
flower. So, I waited. I watched blue-blooded
Adam sleeping soundly

as a trust fund, studied his asymmetrical bone-ladder.
I thought then to take the lower rib's mirror,
to make someone else from him
for me. Hand sweaty, I gripped a talon
I swiped from a dead condor, its great wings
like a book left open by an interrupted
scholar, but Adam awoke
into his strength, yawning out his morning
stink, and I twisted the talon
into my hair to hold it out
of my eyes, focused now.

BOOK II

Dreams? They were strictly unnecessary
in the Garden where everything grew
wild as need, but dreams
were where I learned how
to another, to imagine like
but unlike, indefinite
from definite: her,
a woman, from me, *the*
woman. She came almost every
night to revise
the premise: God created
a woman and then
another one. Just the two
of us, by some craven
blessing. But in dreams,
she was a secret that whooped
in a cave about which
Adam didn't know
and to which I'd sneak
whenever he was off
to name the animals
Not-Human
as if—ha!—we'd swallowed
our beastly
instincts like melonless
seeds. Other times, she was me
and I, Adam. I rose like a wave
at her touch before tiding
back to a smooth dune, nerves
shivering like sea
oats in a storm. Yes, I believe.

I believe in God
the voyeur, who gave
me dreams to cover the dark
valley of my loneliness
with wildflowering
mosquitos. Before I awoke,
I fed her the walnut meat
of my ankle, the cloudmilk
of my breast. I named her
in order to fill my mouth,
famished as I was, force-fed raspberries
until I could swallow little else.

BOOK III

Not halves of a whole.
Not mirrors. Not puzzled
together in the missionary
position. Not a gunpowder
keg and a gun going off.
You scoff, but I wasn't
the fruit to his pit,
a tangle for his nit.
No, Adam and I,
we were more
like brothers
from our quickchange
infancy forward. Big-footed
babies with steel wool
scrubbing our pits,
our groins. His face a full
burning bush. Unpleasant
to kiss. My peached
upper lip rubbed raw
by indifference. I flexed
my bicep in the wellspring
pool. God said, *For godsakes,*
don't name the animals
if you're going
to eat them. The slaughter
will be harder.
(He would know,
I know now.)
Adam named the one that stood
on his foot, *Cow.*
I called her *Tallulah.*

I burned her dried dung
for a cook fire.
But I didn't know how
to cook. I had no mother
to teach me
her bridewell.
Adam was, for all intents
and purposes, my beard—
always dripping
with juice. Always
saving some for later.
But by him, I had citizenship
in the country
where I watched
eagles knot themselves
in spitfire aerials.
If you think about it,
we were the first
domestic animals.
I wore a collar of black-eyed
Susans, and so did Adam.
We were as different
as we weren't. *Who desires
who doesn't?*
I asked, shoving mint
into his mouth.

BOOK IV

Woman always settled
on me like snow
on warm ground. Briefly.
Some mayfly
tender. But my body's weirder
than archetype, more
pulsed than
perfection. If I had been
marble, I would have
lost interest.
Who says Adam's
manlier?
Who became my nickname
for God.
I also called him
When, *What*, and *Where*.
Why just two
of us? Why does Adam
have nipples
if he can't provide
for his children?
How do I unsilly
a never-asked
question?
How do I make silence
my gender?

BOOK V

Adam never forced
himself on me,
not like you are
thinking. Not like God
forced the trumpet-blooming
world upon us, made
an institution of my dewclaw
loneliness. From it,
I was meant to make
my heart a whale
song sung before whales
legged into the ocean,
a tree planted from an un-
imagined seed. I once
asked God the *which*
came first question
but he only answered
by taking
out his pencil
eraser to the concept
drawing. He was Adam's
friend. Not mine.
I had no belly button.
And I never learned the world
by putting it in
my mouth. I was never
a baby in the literal
sense. That's what made childbirth
so painful after we were sent
packing—the shock
of seeing tiny, potatoed

humans like the ego's
root. I think God thought
Adam and I would talk
about everything
but what was there
to say
until I had to
make *no*?

BOOK VI

My brain expanded
like yeast dough
proofing in a covered
bowl. I began
on my hands
and knees, but soon
slouched like a willow.
Eventually, my spine
was as straight
as the definition
narrow. And God shook out
the pterodactyl
like a wet umbrella.
Inside out, it became
the mute swan—
I didn't dare feed it
crumbs from my open
palm, but I watched
it double-s over
the wellspring pond,
and this was the first
moment
I realized there could be
more than one
of anything, the swan
and anti-swan
in symmetry,
imperfect only
for the ripples
glassing away
from its body.

God made man
in his own image,
so they say.
So I made a beloved
in mine.

BOOK VII

Of nakedness I was never
ashamed. Of shame I was never
naked. I never sought
the figtree's shadow
or its briefleaf. Adam clothed me
in want when I refused
his bodygrief. And when he had me
(I knew my duty)
he clothed me
in a cloak of dried bees,
stinger-stitched. I was a Christmas
cactus, my blood bright
flowering. My desert-making
want evaporated
from my tongue as *if*.
As if my teeth could flint
heavens from earth,
water from land,
woman from man,
woman from woman.
Don't think the Garden
was perfect. My feet were calloused
there just the same
as the cast-out lands.
Thorns always pricked.
(I was lonely.)
From his teeth
Adam fishboned meat.

BOOK VIII

How to make a name
from no language, a language from no
name: harness it
to the oxen
body, make your tongue
a blunt plow. The first word
that wasn't God-
given was what I called
her—*Stranger*,
which could be translated
in your tongue
as *The One Who Never
Dies*. I learned to
write by watching
the orbweaver
rubiks her imperfect
mirror, the light
the first flies she ever
caught, all wings.
And, still, her hunger.
Still, the waiting.
The first almond blossoms
curled like magician's fingers
over the lost bronze
coins. Who says it had to be
fruit I took from the tree?
The centuries have been
playing a game
of telephone. I know everything
you know,
by now. I know God

hurled the Garden's key
into the sun. But, back
then, the forbidden
tree grew like the future—
wild as alternate
endings, as a conspiracy
of meanings. This is
not a happy
story. No, this is not
a story at all.

BOOK IX

"If it weren't for the sins the holy book would've been / smaller."
—MAHMOUD DARWISH, "STATE OF SIEGE"
(TRANS. FADY JOUDAH)

The tree I found on a hill
crown-crusted with daffodils
that always annoyed me—all beak,
too cheery. I only meant to take
the shade, as the world was still
fresh from the bake. Its morning
breath Santa Anaed in,
hot and smelling
of sulfur and smoked cheese.
Still, I rested there.
The apocalypse was coming
sooner or later, and I'd need
my energy to survive
my survival, its unending
variations on a theme,
the serpentine chromatics
of blame. I unwrapped my fig
and chèvre sandwich, redacting
the minutes, bite by bite-shaped
bite, until she unfolded
herself from the blistering
noon light, split into three
dimensions by a prism
of want. And then she looked
at me as if we shared an inside
joke and let down
her hair, which was a shadow.
Which was lifedeath.

I was so surprised I forgot to show
don't tell. I forgot
my name means just before
night, the night before
day. I burned *yes* like sage
on the tongue of flame
in my mouth. But the fruit
I plucked? It was peachflesh
muscled in my cage.

BOOK X

The cypresses reached the clouds. The clouds ran
like stockings. The cypresses seemed
to woodfeather the roof
of my mouth when I was elsewhere
benerved. What I called my pleasure:
Elsewhere here. Her mouth
on me: *tangerine pulp.* Words came
as ants synapsing to syrup. Each,
inadequate. Each, everything. She gave me
her tongue. She gave me a way
to refuse and a way to *yes* the world
in brisk barter. She gave me the sweetmeats
of power surrendered
and power offered. The Garden was prolific
in wild invasives. Yes, in knowledge—
I made a kudzu rope
to bind my wrists
to my desire
and to unbind my future
from a pluperfect past. The tense
present in *I am without I am.*
I believe in God as a knot
that knows how to untie itself.
From this new knowledge, a secret fruited
known as a bruise
to thumb the touch apparent.

BOOK XI

To flounder in flora, full-tongued
fucking—those were my Edenic mornings
while Adam lashed himself to the mast
of duty, plugging his ears with bees-
wax so he couldn't hear the echoes
of his failures plumping in the valley.
Yes, he ignored us.
At first. And then came the pressure
from Daddy to name me
like all other animals, *man's*.
And what he did not possess
Adam purchased
with sinewed currency, the buff spiders
of his hands pulling me by the hair
away from the tree into a future
like a contract on which I did not sign
my name. *Forgery*, he called me,
taking personal offense that his rib
made an Other. What is betrayal
except a lack
of control? I asked, and he was beautiful then
the way cliffs are beautiful when you're looking
into a void. You made me
do this, he said, and then I lunged and bit the apple
in his throat, drawing blood
in toothshapes. The second violence.
His eyes flared like salt
thrown into a flame, and then his face
cooled, like lava
into rock. That's when he went to take
for himself the fruit—
to blight my want.

BOOK XII

Exile is first
a condition of a

mirror
surface that is first

a condition of a

need
to see anything

other

than the Other
but of

course to see

oneself as I

saw myself in
the collected

water is to see
another. The

Garden was
the first

border. God, the first

war.

What words
she taught

me evaporated
from my

tongue like the

blood
of a sunflown

dove. No one

can exile
me from

desire, not

even
desire. The road

is hard because
it does

not exist
yet—

Yet I have
collected

thorns in my
cheek, waiting

for Adam's kiss

like the ugly pucker
of a navel

orange I section

to slipfeed the

lyric—all
I smuggled

out besides

knowledge and touch-
memory. This

lyric, little

red-eyed, unnamed
animal

I hide

in my
pocket

above

my clothèd
breast

collapses

the past and the

future
like the atom

bomb or like

flesh

startling
flesh.

2

WIFI NETWORK CALLED "SAD :-("

I.

Oh, I've tried to
        connect before—

    but I don't

    have the password, don't
have even a sense
        from where it's broadcast

        in my building or

which neighbor I never
        speak to has added this

        to our exquisite
        list:

                🛜 PRIMUS SUCKS
                🛜 Church of the Operating Room

—Googled: a Dr. Octagon lyric—

                🛜 Glowing Skin Guest
                🛜 🛢🔪🧻
                🛜 FBI surveillance van

        or the other multitudes
of factory digits, and then mine—

                🛜 FromHere

—my ex's design, the chestnut in
                    here is everywhere
                            everywhere is...

2.

              I know the heaviness

        of their steps: the heft
                    of particular work

boots or one's light sprint. I live
        in unit 1, closest

              to the stairs, the front
                    door, and the brass
                          mailboxes original

              to the building built
              to house nuns training
              to be nurses. They were

                    as I am

walking distance to the hospital

                    where I went for a concussion
                          after mason jars full
                    of things like rice and oatmeal
                                fell from the top of my fridge

                    and hit me on the forehead, right

at my hairline.
        An avoidable blunder. I didn't yell
                or fall, only staggered backward. Quinoa

beading across the floor

and cornmeal caking in my dog's water bowl.

I called someone across town
                    to come and get me.

3.

I got it in the divorce,
                    the router. His 13-character
            password written on a scrap

of paper taped to the side.
            Blue pen.

                    For what am I searching
                    on a network named by an old love?

                    And can I even call him that
                    now that I know I love femmes?

            (I like to believe
                    I have changed
                            rather than hidden—

            but it's probably a combination.)
                    Each

night, I lock the door and slide
                    the chain. Without
        the white noise of the air

                    conditioner, the dog barks
        whenever a neighbor
                    comes home late. Alone

in bed, before I can't
    sleep, I fill my eyes

          with blue light, a signal
to the brain
        to rise. The weighted

blanket, a human
            conceit.

"HEY, GOOGLE, PLAY RAIN SOUNDS"

Play Black Forest birds. Play rainforest frogs.
Play cliffside ocean. Lake lapping at the dock.
Play mountain streams. Play Tibetan bowls.
Siberian blizzard. Logs burning down to coals.

Play summer dusk in Tennessee. Swiss honeybees
at the hive. Cracks forming in a glacier. The dead
dog's heartbeat alive. Play humpback whales.
An underwater dive. Play my sleepless mother.

"A Home in the Meadow," my lullaby. Play
a lava vent near Mount Vesuvius. Play snowmelt.
Play carillons at Christmas. Play my father's step
returning from third shift. Play a city in a pandemic.

Play a stampede of wild mustangs. A steam
engine carriage. Play a teakettle's scream. A flock of sheep
wearing bells. Play throat-singing monks.
Play drizzle on tarp. Play my grandmother's slow clock.

Play Niagara falls. TV static. Play rolling thunder.
A squirrel in the attic. Play the oak's branches in a storm.
Play handbells and choirs. Play the revolution of tires.
Play seven-year cicadas and the muffled voices

of the neighbors. Play Old Faithful. Play distant
interstate traffic. Play the hum of the refrigerator.
Coffee shop talk. Play the local high school's drumline
echoing off of buildings for blocks. Play wheatfields

in wind. Play knitting needles. Footsteps on gravel.
Play cargo train whistles. Play the local classical
station at two a.m. Play the inside of a conch.
Play Bach. Play the gas stove's blue flame and cauterize

the thought. Put me to sleep. Ease me
when I can't. Pack into my ears noise like salt.
Play her breathing next to me, asleep. Play again
the whisper on her lips I couldn't quite understand.

YOU ASK ME TO WRITE ABOUT JOY

The ice on my tongue melts so I place
on my tongue another piece of ice. I am
my habits. I forget you don't like

me to kiss the fruit-flesh root
of your ear with my cold lips. I forget
sadness isn't a personality or even that

it doesn't have to grow in the late light
like a shadow. Sometimes the dark is
bats. Sometimes I close my eyes

like I'm making a bed. That routine
formality. *Open the curtains*, you say
every morning when you wake

in the butterfly shape of our heat.
Open this jar for me, you ask of my small hands
you lend the strength of Atlas.

Poet, do not eat your heart
like a brined & pitted olive.
Hunger is a spoon polished to mirror

the mouth. Behind one front tooth
is an enamel growth my dentist calls
a *pearl*. My tongue worries it

into a miracle. The ignored collard
greens in the garden became yellow
flowers. But we left the leaves

all winter to keep the bees warm.
Could grief do the same for joy?

MY BED WAS BELOW A PAINTING OF THE RAPE OF IO

Midnight sun. No curtains,
   only red, yellow, green,
     and purple construction
       paper I'd taped (masking)

         the windows. In a squint:
         stained glass. I slept in fits—
thirty minutes broken

by hours staring, hours
masturbating, and hours
   rereading sentences
     I couldn't remember

       reading. The moon, something
        like a cheek smudge left on
     a window by a train

      passenger. I left my
   body. I sucked black pepper
candies at my desk, took shots
   of Brennivín in the shared

      kitchen with the other
      artists. Volcanic ash
         blew in and grayed

      my black jeans drying
   on the line. No rain
since April. Now June,
near solstice. A new species

of biting flies erupted
    one night in the bedrooms.
        New birds from Greenland.

        New birds from Britain.
    New birds shitting
    seeds of new plants scrabbling
in the ash. The hottest

summer on Iceland's
    record. I stopped writing
        with pen. I stopped

        typing in the word
            processor, that work
    of making a light
    slightly darker. Instead,

    I took lipstick
and traced my cheek
    scar, pressing it like a kiss

        on paper. I called this
        a poem. I laid awake
            in my underwear, upside
        down in bed, to stare

        at the black lines
    of the heifer, the curly-haired
god. They never

    broke, their figures
        a knot. A man's work,
        I was sure. I had been
            here before. Not as in

déjà vu. Not here here.
But in the country.
Snowed-in. Another season

with a drunk husband,
an unheeded *no*. New
birds from Greenland.
Birds from Britain.

Old seeds finally sown.
I called him to say
I was coming home

soon but not to
him. Those last nights
I'd walk the lake
against the wind.

ARCADIA

What wagers one in return—
         palm-warm raisins, further

goldened by sweat-prismed
         sun—for entrance at its border?

Doubtless: an immolation
         of the soul, lighter fluid

squeezed on as if this were
         some briquette barbecue

scourging a dandelioned
         lawn. No, think more rose petals

& stinging nettle, stones
         hardened by the pressure

of ruin, or light like a cymbal
         crash, a cache of river pearls—

not a plastic basket of strawberries
         displayed beside squirty whip

cream & film-wrapped pound
         cake. Not hotel soaps that claim

to be made of goat's milk
         & vetiver. What barter can be made

between a god who wields
         a lightning bolt & another,

a radio wave? You heard
　　　your ancestors speaking

to you through a game
　　　of telephone, saying *Bring*

us the future. When they really
　　　said, *Leave us alone.*

FRENCH HORN

Approximate in plastic, one-somethingth
in scale, you flatulated *yays* when I

long lipped you, playing Gabriel's shadow
over the ceramic holy family

painted in Easter pink, blue, and yellow.
No keys, only change in embouchure—puffs

of air like burrs in my Memaw's ear. *Can
you take that somewhere, sugar?* Your gold

paint flecking off under a fingernail.
I breathed into you life beyond decor-

ation, your place on the artificial
balsam bare. In the strawberry-themed

kitchen, I'd *Lo!* you as a staticky ice
skater gained speed on the aerial

& roar as they lifted into
a double Axel. Every Xmas Eve,

I volunteered to read the scripture
for the whole family, who should have known

by then I was prone to annunciation.
Hark! you cried for me, using my air.

IN THE EXIT VESTIBULE OF THE LEPIDOPTERARIUM

On the second glass,
            a decal—   *STOP*
                    until the attendant indicates it is safe
                            to proceed

—but my beloved tried to push on, shouldering the crash bar,
oblivious to instruction, just as a toddler
                    slipped in the first door,
        ahead of his stroller and mother,
                            a blue-winged thing no bigger
            than his hand
    kiting in, on his draft. An accident?
                    An escape?

        Wait! I said
—as *Stop*, the attendant—

            to my beloved, who turned, letting
                    the door click
    shut behind her

as the stroller dozed in,
            the mother telling the boy,

                            Look! One followed you!

                Then, almost apologetic: *Maybe*
                            it will go
        back inside on its own.

    The four of us, standing at different
            points but looking in the same

    direction:

the attendant, now with a handled net
grabbed from a hook on the wall, eyeing

the butterfly, blue as the coldest planets,
as frostbite on fingers, fluttering near the ceiling

like a word just on the tip
                    of the tongue. I had never

seen a butterfly net before, only in cartoons
                    and old photographs of Nabokov, where he looked

unhappy in his joy.   The attendant swung—

        all of us following
direction to stay and watch this   fleeting other
                    trapped; in human

                    order, placed back.

GOLDEN AGE

In a time before wars
there were wars

elsewhere, just
as there were
rotting mulberries

because there
were too many
and not enough

birds because the wars
we needed and the wars
were boredoms

which have never favored
speechless others

or the diplomacy
of distance, a borderless

country in which
arrowshafts
are quick-changed
currency. There

is no such thing
as allegory,

not when men make
of their hands calluses.

LATE NIGHT CLASSICAL RADIO HOST

The first thing you need is a voice.
One someone can fall asleep to.
Can sleep through. Words
twinkling in faint starbursts
of static. Your timbre must sotto
the way a library book smells
like the mausoleum of Erato.
You must bring a thermos—
an old metal one, dinged.
Fill it with quote-unquote
coffee but drink
slowly. Before three, you'll have to
say Saint-Saëns without slurring.
Oh, and you'll need to know Italian,
of course. Or, at least, how to pronounce
it—those hard Cs in *concerti*.
When you arrive, take off winter
and hang it on the hook
by the door. Your wool
socks on the ancient green
carpet will remind you of a long-ago
dream in which you were an army
of one marching across Elysia.
The studio's wood paneling
will one day give you a splinter
you'll suck out during
the flute *minuet* of Bizet's
"L'Arlésienne Suite No. 2."
You'll get used to the schedule
of sleeping through the day,
only to wake as the sun sets
like a bald man's head
under a hat. You'll prepare for your shift
by stuffing cotton balls

in your mouth and saying *catgut lute*
five times fast.
You'll do this because you know
there are only a few
who'll listen to you.
And this, you think,
is good practice
for after death.

MAGICAL REALISM

The autopsy determined
the cause of death
was the impossibility of being
alive with a wasp's nest
spit-pottered around
the heart. The coroner couldn't understand
how a man could live
for so many pages, pulse charted
with regular punctuation,
with this condition with which
no one else had
ever been born
or borne into
death. The most logical
among the village
said a stinger
had been absorbed
into his bloodstream
when he failed
to suck it out from the back
of his hand sticky
with pomegranate
juice, his teeth
seeded black. Others shouted
malediction and poured
smoke into his grave
so that they could see
if the spirit
ascended. But they witnessed
only the serpentine
unknotting of their own
grief into superstition,
the ghost that moans
in mouths
of the living.

THIS POEM HAS BEEN MINED FOR DATA

—for DJF especially, and the following cohort

1.

Another degree
        candidate in   my office—

they don't want
        to submit   their thesis

to the data-   base.
        The electronic submission

requirement, ubiquitous;
        the vendor,   for profit.

For weeks, they've gone
        back   and forth with

the formatting
        coordinator,   who makes

sure the poems
        are machine   legible. One

student suggests
        a new ms.   but whatever

they submit   teaches—

2.

Before book, before
        glue, before
        ink tire-
                        tracked
        on treepulp,

this was light,
        or rendered
in it,
                        to me, my blinking
eye
catching a blinking
line
        where I left
                off, where my thought
        stopped, where
                        the language
                                paused like prey
        hearing a rustle

in the brush, when
        I ought to see

        the Doc's *Saving*

dot dot dot—

        the bots
                crawling
        my song,
                like note-fat
        ticks on
                a stave.

3.

One student suggests
        adding in false statements to his
document,

        if it's already going to be
attached to his name:
                e.g., *"I like blueberry yogurt,"* something he hates.

        (Like feeding the incessant
                barking
        a steak
                injected with antifreeze.)

        And I agree:
Poems *are* valuable—
                        (cynically, I think:)
                                not as is—
                        but as venture
                                        capital.

4.

An analogy:

> trees have many
> species, casting
> different shadows
> that are still
> recognizable as
> "tree shadow."
>
> One could
> gather any
> leaves from
> as many
> species as one
> likes and
> combine them
> to create
> "tree shadow."

Thus,

> a poem is one
> grammar for
> <ref="poem">.

TRAGIC HERO

You have to pass a physical
in which the physician-poets

focus on locating your fatal
flaw. A rage that emerges

quick as a crocus?
Or: a heel like the soft part

of a baby's skull?
Or: a love as obsessive

as a mosquito? Don't
try to ameliorate

your diagnosis, the signature
binding you to a cameo in a future

hero's trek down into
the Underworld where your shade

will be porcupined
with arrows. Wrench out as many as

you like from the darkness
you once called your *chest, buttocks,*

or *thigh*—you'll never
remove a single one.

Not even the one in your eye.

LION PAINTED BY SOMEONE WHO HAS NEVER SEEN A LION

You, dog-bodied ape

face. You, orangutangonal quadruped with legs

lamb-bent, your lip almost aquiver, your brow in tectonic

contortions above your precious metal

eyes focused on Saint Jerome, who plucked

from your paw your wildness, your roam.

In this evolutionary mastication, you're hog sized, ribs scythed, starved

for attention, for a human hand in your Samsonian

mane—or maybe a comb.

ANTEDILUVIAN

No one remembers
the preceding
drought, the way the ground
cracked into terrestrial
lightning or how one
might awake
in the night thinking
your husband so close
you could feel his
breath, his eyelashes on your
cheek, only to reach
up and dust away a lichen-
colored moth, thirsty
for dream
tears. And it's true: I had so many
nightmares then—
I blame the sky,
where the water gathered
its dark skirts,
brushing so low
the treetops were faceless
like our ancestors.
The Earth didn't have
such deep pockets
then. The water
hadn't had time to bore
its way into
bedrock. And so God
evaporated it all
into a storm that wouldn't
break, stagnant
as my grandmother's yolked
eye. As my husband cut
trees, I'd wait

for their leaves
quartzed
with condensation.
I'd lick them
as if they were
spoons. He knew
all the animals,
except the two
by two, would
drown, and so
he charted the food
chain, slaughtering
for salt. This job
he gave to me.
And I know why:
he wanted me more
thirsty
for doom.

DILUVIAN

We waited in the ark's
cabin, barrels
on the deck to collect
the long-withheld
rain. We listened to it
as if for a heartbeat
at a dead man's chest.
And, finally, they came.
I could not
see them, and Noah
told me they weren't
there, they *weren't*—
but I could hear
their fists against
the hull, nails
ravaging the wood
like animal claws
before we were
lifted, the first swell
like a dizzy spell
when one stands up
too quick. And then
the rush caught
the whole and we were
carried forward. Noah said
some had found a way
to hold on, but he beat
their fingers with a spare
plank until they let
go. I stayed
below as I was
told, sick rising
up like suspicion.
I slept when I wasn't

retching, my dreams
full of lions
savaging their cubs.

COVENANT

No words could
describe the
sounds, no
unvoweled
onomatopoeia
could capture
the animals'
distress, the giraffes
kneeling like
lambs, unable
to stand, necks
boaed around
their tiny
enclosure.
Sometimes
I'd take out
the mice
and hide them
in my dress
pocket where
they'd fit
themselves
together
like the dark
and bright
sides of a half
moon. This,
their whiskered
movements
just above
my breast,
gave me
the sense
I was living

in a body
again, something
lost to me
when I boarded
the extinction.
Before, I kept
begging
Noah to build
slower, much
slower, to never
finish, to save
the world
by never
hammering
the last nail
into the ark. What
did I know,
he wondered
aloud. I was
just a vessel,
like the ship. The new
mother
to the world—
and to it,
to God and
to my husband,
like the animals—
captive stock.

POSTDILUVIAN

The ark lowered
like a body into a grave.
But before it came
to rest, I could
hear things knocking
bluntly against
the hull. Debris—
a new word
for people, homes,
animals. Noah kept
the dove as a pet,
feeding it a pinch
of nibbles
whenever it cooed
in his ear. He asked me
over and over why I
didn't coo in his ear, too—
he'd saved me
after all. I never responded,
dragging some poor soul
by the ankles
into the compost pile.
The renewed world
smelled like death
with a fishy undertone.
So many had swum
so far, only to be left
in the mud. I dried
them in the sun,
ground their bones
into a fine powder
to sprinkle over
the garden. I was
raped every night

after our meager
meals. The wolves
would howl
in their cages
whenever they heard
the slap of flesh,
Noah's grunts
like glottaled
alephs, and after
he was finished,
he'd call the dove
down from its perch,
hold a seed between
his lips and let the bird
take it. He called this
a kiss. He called this
love. We let
the herbivores go
first, let them
propagate
before we released
the predators.
That night, I watched them
run in pairs
into the distance,
planting their
prints into the soggy
earth, knowing
their savagery
innocent.

3

NONBINARY BIRD OF PARADISE

Unplumed, my crown.
    Better
        an imitate-bouquet
    ochred by sunshowers

sieved by the dream-green
    canopy
        oceaning above
    the forest floor cleared

of debris. With drab-
    throated
        laughter, I govern
    your eye, yellow like

the rings of Saturn. My
    oilslick
        feathers fan—
    as if to engorge

a fire. O, I
    practiced
        in front of a mirror—
    Would you stay

& watch me, even
    though
        I have no blue velvet
    skirt or ruby-raw
throat? Would you
    brandish
        at the encroaching, sequined
    egos your bright beak

like a sword—?

I CALLED MYSELF *MONSTER*

When I slept
with men, they'd play

with my nipples
as if they were using

a rotary phone,

dialing
0 over &

over, the

operator never
answering, never

connecting

the lines. I
learned the lie
of annunciation,

of birdsong
before dawn. Of

citrus in winter,
that bitter

sugar. Of the open
war

which was a
door

I'd stand
in, keys in

hand,

      two
      pitbulls

      enleashed

      with the idea
      of snakes—

One man's

    eyes
    sizzled

      like coins
      of lava

      in a
      fountain

    as I
    left to

return to
leave

      again, like

      an angel
      pardoned

      or a dormant

perennial.

Black-eyed
Susan.

Jonquil.

Some riddles
come

undone

in the telling—
My neck

burned,

light
like a squeeze

of lemon.

My hair
maned

by the wind,

I called

myself
monster

gathering all

the world's

animals in my
heart's pen.

I'M NOT JEALOUS YOU'RE DANCING WITH SOMEONE ELSE

Usually I dance like a paper
                    airplane sailed
          toward a crush
                    only to dogleg

at the last minute and peck
                    the stubbled neck
          of an unintended
                    consequence, whereas

you are like flambé leaping
                    to catch
          the whole room
                    on fire. I see you

lazy-Susan your booty over
                    into someone else's
          Elvis pelvis. But I don't
                    feel as if I've swallowed

an ice cube whole—not
                    anymore—and I don't
          make a move
                    to cut in. Instead I rise

on your heat draft like I'm no
                    ordinary glider but
          something untethered,
                    an origami condor.

ECHO EYES HERSELF

With a thunderhead pompadour
                     I dive, gaze first, into the pool,

reckless after Narcissus. Juno's curse
                     lifted easily as a skirt

once I realized everything's been
                     said before. Besides, even when I couldn't

say anything that hadn't been
                     said, sentences still built themselves

inside my head like Escheresque
                     staircases, leading nowhere

& everywhere all at once. I see myself
                     now as someone else would, as a foot

sees a footprint. The sun sees
                     what it illumines. I pout and mouth

the word *pout*. I would never drown
                     here. To see oneself one has to look

at the water. To look into
                     it, you've gone too far.

GENDER REVEAL PARTY

We're having a mirror!
                    A mirror facing a mirror!
          It's a marble
                    statue, a neoclassical copy—

all its appendages broken
                    off like stale baguettes!
          We're having a three-tier cake
                    with Marilyn Monroe inside!

We're having "Happy
                    Birthday, Mr. President"!
          We're having a scandal!
                    A child of Zeus!

A demi-deity with rings
                    on their fingers! We're having
          a kumquat! A kiwi! A cantaloupe!
                    We're having an argument!

A lie-down! A little shut-eye!
                    We're having sleep paralysis!
          A pins-and-needles
                    feeling in the feet!

Just what we wanted!
                    We're having a dachshund
          on a rollerskate! A word
                    that sounds offensive

in another language!
                    We're having a cigarette
          after sex! We're having it!
                    Like once or twice

a week! We're having

         an earworm! A hook!

    We're baiting it!

       We're having the champagne!

The turducken! We're splitting it!

         We're having a custody battle!

    Already!

       We're pretty sure

we're having misgivings!

         We're having a scratch-off!

    A new car

      on *The Price*

Is Right! We're having our ears

         candled! Our bread buttered!

    A strawberry!

       A rally! A fossil! An unutterable.

"SIR"

It had been so long since someone called
me that, the word like hot iron could be
bent into a blunt scythe by my hammering

heart. I answered to
it and did not

correct the teenager behind the fast
food counter, for though it slashed
at me, it did not cut. Years ago,
I would have gone home
in tears, convinced I wasn't pretty

enough. *Feminine*
enough, whatever

that means. But I only went to grab my box
of chicken and the teenager then said,

Oh my god, I'm so sorry
—MA'AM.

Both words like two sounds
at the same frequency—

so loud both and neither
can be heard.

ANTI-DOMESTIC

The night before, a sleeping bag
on the floor, body aches in a constellation

of gravity. All my things gone
to another city.   (With him.)

(Except my desire.)   She came in
the morning with coffees, the half-and-half

split & floating. We talked
about our husbands, the island between us.

I knew if I moved closer to her
I would move   closer to her.

But language performed
its function: we said what we wanted

by not saying it, circling it
as if it was a fire. This was before

we were   against the wall
in the laundry room where I once & many

times lifted his wet clothes (heavier
than they had seemed, than they had

been before, & darker) from washer
to dryer.   Her leather jacket

creaking as she raised her arms
to pull my hair. A teacher

once had me write a poem about something
that wasn't sexy, in a sexy way.

(Washing dishes? Doing laundry?)

The rest of my life
I have been unlearning.

EMILIA, WIDOW TO IAGO

I dodged the dagger. I feigned my death
until the influentials with the lieutenant
left. I gathered my things, goatherded
my thoughts. I tied around my wounds
linen knots. My mistress—a lamb
with a woolen heart. The first step?
Like emerging from a thundercloud
into a desert. I could hear my heart beat like it had
never. A frantic fly inside a dead man's cheek.
(That fucker.) I peeked down the hall. This way and that.
Padded to the door. I was born into the world in a caul
of disrespect. No one would look for my corpse.
Except to make a joke about bad divorce.
And stick around here? Not to be the rag and mop.

DAPHNE, FELLED

The first blow came like an icepick
                headache. And the second?
      Like a weakness in the knees.

I still remember what it was like
                having a human body, a woman's
      body. Full of rage, of honeybees

stinging each fingertip from the inside
                out while the drones busied
      in my heart, wings scraping

the spongey interior of my lungs
                while I ran from that dung-stain
      of a god. I lowercase his need.

I blot it out with my shade
                as if he were a weed. I can
      only remember my old body

through this one, now leaning,
                now falling in a fragrant
      crush of leaves, a rustle

like a prayer reaching the mind
                of a god. There are many
      gods to whom one should

never pray. Women especially,
                hear me. If I had fallen with no one
      around, I still would have

made a sound. Through me,
                winds have screamed all the way
      into eternity.

MY GENDER

Is a tree falling in a forest
with no one around to hear it.

Is a rhetorical question. Is negative
capability.

Is a bull who can't see red.

Is a matador who forgot to wear clothes
in a dream.

Is a solve-for-x equation.

Is glacier melt.

Is cinders threaded through
an ice needle.

Is a narwhal skeleton hanging from the ceiling
of the museum of natural history.

Is confirmation bias.
Is proving ground.

Is fruit with a rind
& soft pulp inside.

Is my childhood cat named Clementine
until she went to be spayed

& instead was neutered.

Is a cat's memory of its first name.

Is the *e* becoming fainter
as the book goes on.

Is a recipe I don't follow.

Is a stop sign I roll through.

Is waking up before my alarm.

Is sleeping through it.

Is drool on my pillow.

Is staring at a mouth
whenever someone is speaking.

Is looking at something
instead of through.

Like a dirty window.

A crescendo.

A flightless bird.

Is a peacock feather willowing
your shoulder blade.

Is a shiver.

Is walking through a spiderweb.

A game of double dutch.

A loose dog without a collar.

An oxbow lake. Bioluminescent algae.

An X on a map.

A proprietary token.

A fox screaming in the night,
mistaken for a woman.

ARTEMIS WEARS A STRAP-ON

Chariot, I am. And six
                golden-antlered stags.

     Legs fuzzed above the knee.

          Below, bee stingers unshaven.

Hands a clamor, I'm a gentle
              archer. Breasts like knots in

rope. A purple scar

       in my thigh-meat, I'll make your heart

beat like all four hooves
             left the ground

    returning, and kiss your ankles—

       walnuts held in a cheek.

What is godlike in you,
             I'll godden. Sudden

    as slag in heat. You, my dogs

       howling. You, my captive

capturing. Thumb on
             the golden raisin until a navel-

    thwang of bowstring.

       My quiver's never

empty. Your kisses like poppies

              petaling. Ruin is

what stands

     the longest. Wonder me.

MY BEARD

My first performance in drag
was at a Bible study

play for children at the orphanage:
I was Abraham, a beard

elasticked around my ears,
a cane mimed with a baseball

bat. Those nights I slept
like a tongue inside a mouth,

unbelieving in anything
except guilt. In the mission

bunkhouse, I could hear
another girl in her sleep

murmur *flamingo*.
And under my pillow

was a leather folder
of CDs, the size of another

pair of shoes in my suitcase.
In two nights, the mission leaders

would call on us to burn
our books, our music—

anything that caused us
to forget god

on his poot of whip cream
in the sky. But I burned

nothing in the fire that night
except my sight.

BECAUSE "LESBIAN ELEPHANTS" IS SO PLEASURABLE TO SAY

I say it in the shower over and over, under
my horse-huff breath, a water droplet
hanging on an eyelash. That brief monocle.

I twist the phrase like the stem of a maraschino
with my tongue. I make cocktails
with it, garnished with iced borage.

I leave my browser tab open on the article.
I hear it in the conch shell key-hider.
In the blips of words between radio

stations. I suck on it like a Werther's
Original. I involve my vocal cords.
I put my ear to the rail of it, as if listening

for a coming train. I feed this earworm
to the birds. I sing it flat. I Gaga.
I Dolly. I Dylan. It would be a good band name.

I would like to record a song that,
played backwards, would say it.
I make it my password. My safe word.

I sleeptalk it. I open it like a parachute
when I jump into the abyss. I blow
my coffee cool with it. I take it apart like clock

to see how it works. If I were a gnat,
I'd say it in ear after ear at the outdoor
revival. Run it like a faucet.

I leave the lights on inside it.
I'm saying the phrase over and over again
in the shower. A branch

of eucalyptus hangs from the showerhead.
If we were lesbian elephants, I would
grab the eucalyptus with my trunk and swat

your great elephant rump. I would drape
my trunk around your shoulders like a boa
constrictor. I would mount you

in the lake at dawn, ankle-deep
in mud. But I am only human
in a herd of words I love.

I TOLD THE MAN WHO YELLED "DON'T YOU WANT TO LOOK LIKE A LADY?" TO FUCK OFF

at which point he came
        toward me, the way a crow slice-wings

past a mockingbird's nest
        or a doomsday asteroid gives our extinction

the slip—I was too quick
        to get inside my car, the gas

pump already re-holstered,
        and lock the doors. At which point he retreated,

flexing his fingers, and I realized
        my keys were on my trunk. A few looks—

one over the lid of an ICEE.
        My body quick to be flushed

into the dark plumbing
        of dissociation, my heart like a cloud

testing its thunder
        in a soundproof room. Soon, everyone

drove away into the heat
        their concern. My engine, cooled.

PEGASUS

Horse muscle strung on   bird bone—a bow cord
on brittle stave. To   strengthen the bird, you

weaken the horse, so   say the physics
of the bolt &, vice   versa, the physics

of flight. Like peach   to lime, two
evolutionary   branches grafted

together. What   tethers the slick wick
of imagination   to the quick burn

of ordered or-   chestration? Pegasus
couldn't fly in Europe   after the conquest

of reason. My last   name means *Phillip's*
son or *lover*   *of horses*, depending

on the language of   origin. Depending
on what mythology   I brand on the rump

of this   plow horse. I am a son
of my father   just as I am his

daughter. Let us say   then, in hopeful
anachronism,   that flying Pegasus

was neither mare nor   stallion.

AT A BARCELONA QUEER CLUB, A MAN ASKS IF YOU WANT TO DANCE WITH SOMEONE MORE MASCULINE THAN ME

I know how to
translate his
body

language, even if
I can't
hear what he is

saying in your
ear. My
Spanish, slow

even when
there's not
a flubbing bass

beat & a
shimmerheat
in my cheeks.
What is this

fear—the
body's
kneeling to the
improbability

of us
surviving
unbothered?
Our cab

                  bet: whoever

                              kisses the other
                              first

            has to—

                              What? (I'll never
                              tell.)

He's too close,

                              & jealousy lights
                              like dry

            grass on a
            cigarette.

                              It's my first time

                  out

                              dancing with
                              you,

with a woman
            ever,

                              my purgatorial

            decade of

                              straight-facing
                              evasion

            done &

                              over. Who am I
                              to want,

            quick as a salt

                              flare, to say
                              something—

                  (not *mine*,
                  except

juntas here)?
Your

hand's bird-
nervous

before you

lace your fingers

with mine

& ask him for
space.

But I'm gay,
you later say

he said, when we
are all

but undressed in
our

room we locked

against the alarm
we

find but forget

in one another,
together.

PANGAEA

Let us imagine all things
more alike there, a there that is now

here & there. Chimeras not
chimeras then, couldn't be

a conflation of things as yet
undifferentiated. In Pangaea, one

led not to two
graves but the open

air. And so, let us admit man
& woman are only corralled

according to cultural
signposts, making them rather

more *strawman*
& *strawwoman*, set apart

by some deterministic sense
of fuzzy genitals,

which were the catholic
occasion for the first human

shrieks that rippled
across the first bodies

of water that all
flowed into one another

at the beginning of the world
as they do still.

NOTES

The Queerness of Eve

In taking on Eve's persona and refiguring her as queer, I hoped to exemplify Adrienne Rich's words from her 1980 essay "Compulsory Heterosexuality and Lesbian Existence": "We may faithfully or ambivalently have obeyed the institution [of heterosexuality], but our feelings—and our sensuality—have not been tamed or contained within it."

In March 2019, I saw *"Pecat original"* ("original sin"), from ca. 1590, at the Frederic Marès Museum in Barcelona. This statue shows three figures: Adam covering his genitals with a fig leaf, Eve holding a round fruit and also covering her genitals, and the "serpent" twining around the tree of knowledge. The serpent is figured as having the body of a snake with the torso and head of a woman who emerges from the crown of foliage. After I saw the work, I knew that it wasn't fruit that Eve claimed; it was her agency, her desire for another woman.

A personal photograph of the altarpiece appears below.

The epigraph for "Book I" comes from Marianne Boruch's book *The Anti-Grief* (Copper Canyon Press, 2019).

The epigraph for "Book IX" comes from Mahmoud Darwish's *The Butterfly's Burden* (Copper Canyon Press, 2006), translated by Fady Joudah.

The form for "Book XII," as well as two other poems in this book, was adapted from a poetic form created by my former MFA student Amy Parkes.

"Lion Painted by Someone Who Has Never Seen a Lion" is for Gregory.

"My Gender" is for Samuel Cormac, after an exercise they assigned as my teaching intern to my Fall 2021 Queer Poetry & Poetics class.

ACKNOWLEDGMENTS

Thank you to the literary journals who originally published these poems:

The Adroit Journal: "Book VII" and "Book X"

American Poetry Review: "Daphne, Felled" and "Lion Painted By Someone Who Has Never Seen a Lion"

The Atlantic: "Late-Night Classical Radio Host"

Blackbird: "Antediluvian," "Diluvian," "Covenant," and "Postdiluvian"

Black Warrior Review: "Book XII"

Copper Nickel: "Book III," "Book IV," "Book VI," and "Book VIII"

EcoTheo Review: "Book V"

Poetry International: "Golden Age"

Snapdragon: "Arcadia," "In the Exit Vestibule of the Lepidopterarium," and "This Poem Has Been Mined for Data"

Southern Humanities Review: "Echo Eyes Herself"

Books are never written in a vacuum. They are born out of reading, conversation, and living.

As such, I have to thank first the person with whom I have created and continue to create a beautiful emotional, intellectual, and creative life. Thank you, Claudia, for writing in the room adjacent to where I was writing many of "The Queerness of Eve" poems. Thank you for letting me read your poems and letting me copyedit your articles. Thank you for having "book clubs" with me about films, podcast episodes, conversations, and even books. Thank you for traveling with me, literally and figuratively, to places I never thought I would go. You have loved me fiercely, uniquely, and expansively. Te amo, te quiero, te adoro.

Secondly, I could have neither written this book nor could I imagine these last few years without Felipe and Elisa. You have shown me what it means to be a family, including all of those intense conversations over dinner. I love you both.

Thanks also to my parents: my mother Janet, my father Ken, and my stepmother Sonia. To those other family members—especially Robin, Jim, Rachael, and Noah—who have continued to love and support me after coming out.

Gracias a todes en la familia Cabello, Hutt, y Güell. Todes me hacen sentir bienvenide. Gracias por su paciencia en mis intentos de hablar chileno.

To those I embrace as family through their embrace of our family, especially Jeremiah Meyer and Kaycee Eckhardt.

To my friends of the heart, especially Gregory Kimbrell, Joey Kingsley, Lena Moses-Schmitt, Rachel Mennies, Tomás Morín, Daniel B. Coleman, Julia Smith, Nicky Beer, Brian Barker, Taneum Bambrick, Jameela Dallis, Maca Urzúa, Trenna Sharpe, Erin Andersen, Sumita Chakraborty, Faye Stewart, Amy Gremillon, Sara Eliza Johnson, Erika Meitner, Gabrielle Calvocoressi, Jenny Johnson, Dana Levin, Diane Seuss, Rebecca Stafford, Tarfia Faizullah, Ross White, Nickole Brown, Ryan Teitman, Julia Teitman, Jo Klein, Suzanne Helms, Nicole Lungerhausen, Sybil Baker, Tracy Tanner, and Georgia Sams.

To my UNCG creative writing colleagues Xhenet Aliu, Stuart Dischell, Holly Goddard Jones, Derek Palacio, and Jessie Van Rheenan, as well as the departments of and people within English and Women's, Gender, and Sexuality Studies, especially Heather Brook Adams, Risa Applegarth, Jen Feather, Jennifer Keith, Lisa Levenstein, Neelofer Qadir, and Jennifer Whitaker. To my Library & Information Science colleague Colin Post and Special Collections & University Archives colleague Stacey Krim. To my Religious Studies colleague Derek Krueger for enthusiastically teaching "The Queerness of Eve" in his Adam and Eve course. To the UNCG AAUP chapter for all your work advocating for our students, colleagues, and programs.

To my students, past and present. You may not know it, but you are collectively some of the most important people in my life.

To my teachers Kathleen Graber and David Wojahn, who have stayed in my life and continue to teach me. To Mary Flinn.

To my editor Mary Biddinger, book designer Amy Freels, and copyeditor Thea Ledendecker—life givers to my book and patient companions to me.

To the staff of Gullkistan Center for Creativity in Laugarvatin, Iceland, where I spent two weeks in June 2019 and Buinho Creative Hub in Messejana, Portugal, where I spent two weeks in June 2022.

To Guilford For All for creating local change. To Scuppernong Books for always being a home for writers and readers.

Lastly, to Natosha and Laurie for supporting me in ways that no one else can.

Photo: Justin Nash

Emilia Phillips (they/them/theirs) is the author of four previous poetry collections from the University of Akron Press, including *Embouchure* (2021), and five chapbooks. Their poetry, creative nonfiction, and book reviews have appeared widely. They are an Associate Professor of Creative Writing in the Department of English; MFA in Writing Program; and the Women's, Gender, and Sexuality Studies Program at UNC Greensboro.